RHYMES
of a Prairie Scot

John L. Fairbairn

McARA PRINTING LIMITED, CALGARY

Published by McAra Printing Limited   Calgary, Alberta

Printed in Canada

Edited by Dorothy Deer

Cover design and illustrations by Merle McKnight

to Mother

Elizabeth Lowry Fairbairn

JOHN L. FAIRBAIRN 1937

I sing not of some leisure stream to paddle,
        No pendant muse doth urge my simple chiming.
I rate not Pegasus to sit astraddle.
        I have no secret love to read my rhyming.
I am no "Rabby" Burns, nor yet a Langdon,
        I just don't drip with golden voice Divine.
I speak in accents slow, and oft' belabored.
        I speak the tongue of this great West of mine.
Through stubble field and slough and big wild yonder.
        I've been away and absence makes the heart
        grow fonder.
Big land, big men, and women fair as sunshine.
        'Tis milk and honey land, land of high adventure.
She's the fairest of ten thousand, and she's mine.

FOREWORD

Throughout his life John Fairbairn displayed a strong sense of perception into the lives of the people he met, He had an uncanny ability to inspire those who were discouraged or depressed. He was a man of feeling, who often provided strength to those around him. His keen observations and sensitivity are revealed in these poems.

John's life story, too, provides some insight into his understanding of human nature. His mother died at the time of his birth at Peterborough, Ontario, on March 23, 1910. Shortly thereafter, his father moved from Peterborough to a farm in the Lloydminister district of Saskatchewan. Here John spent his childhood in a nature setting, and frequently spoke of the hikes he took with his step-mother, often gathering mushrooms by the bucket.

As a boy, John was religiously inclined. He was told his own mother hoped her son would become a minister. He became good friends with the Anglican minister, Canon Freeman, and enjoyed starting the fires each Sunday morning in the little country church near Lloydminster. Their friendship continued over the years. Later in life, John himself spent six years in the church ministry.

John left home in his early teens to make a life for himself. His strong desire to improve his status through his extensive reading, his search for knowledge and his keen interest in people, gave him much needed strength and courage.

He could tell fascinating stories of his colorful experiences during the depression years when he travelled the freight cars from province to province, sometimes stopping off long enough to sharpen scissors and knives for the price of a meal. He made some fast friends among his freight car companions, but also told of frightening experiences when confronted with dangerous criminals sharing the same freight car.

It was a point of great pride that while he was reciting poetry to a gathering of people, the widow of Sir Wilfred Laurier, former Prime Minister of Canada, invited him to recite at her home for her lady guests. This event was the beginning of a warm friendship between them.

The author spent more than 30 years in the photographic business, and is well known as a portrait photographer to many Canadians. After World War II, he owned the Child's Studio at Windsor, Ontario, with branches at Chatham and London. The work of this studio took him to most parts of Ontario. He owned the D'Angelo Portrait Studio in Calgary from 1965 to retirement early in 1973.

Depression days prevented the author from publishing his poems in the early 1940's. But, upon retiring in 1973, he began the preparation to have RHYMES OF A PRAIRIE SCOT published. Since he passed away before he finished the project, his wife, daughter, and friends carried the task to completion.

Although he inspired and uplifted the lives of many people, one of the most grateful was a blind friend, Irene Thompson. He spent many hours attempting to restore her faith and will to live after the sudden loss of her sight. It seems appropriate to end this book with her expression of gratitude which is representative of the gratitude of hundreds of people who were inspired by the author.

CONTENTS

Prairie Wool

PATRIOTISM

REFLECTIONS

Love

A SMILE

If I can smile, there is no cause for Fear.
I know that I am rich beyond compare
Though I am dressed in clothes all patched and rough,
While sun shines down, I know that God is near.

For God is love and love will bring a smile,
When we can smile the clouds all roll away;
The mists all vanish with the early dawn,
And then we must admit that life's worthwhile.

What matter if I have no gold to give,
For gold means nought if one can give a smile.
If there's a smile within my heart, I know
That I can help some struggling soul to live.

(August 15, 1934)

A GIFT FOR YOU

I cannot give you gold rich-set with jewels,
No clustered diamonds of a deep blue-white.
I cannot give you robes of shimmering silk,
Or violets, deep and velvety as dark of night.

My gift will add no beauty to your home,
Among the brighter gifts 'twill not be seen,
But what I offer will be swathed in hope,
And nurtured on the breath of heaven's dream.

The world may deem it just a boyish whim,
And some may turn to muffled scornful jeers;
But you will know my humble little gift
Was bathed to purety by lonely years.

Should you accept, then life for me will start,
The gift I offer is my love, my heart.

(October 27, 1940)

PASSING LOVE

As leaping waters in the Spring
Dash up to greet the morning sun,
Where sunbeams stop to dance and sing,
As bright sunbeams have always done;
As singing lark up in the sky
Would usher in the day anew,
As little breezes joyfully sigh,
And kiss the rose all wet with dew;
As would the lily in pure bliss
Hold to its lips a drop of rain
Thus would I greet you with a kiss,
My love, if we should meet again.

FEET OF CLAY

I'd like to write a melody of Spring
With tender kisses from a shower of rain;
But I can never find the time for such,
The summer fallow's ready for the grain.

I'd like to pen a poem to the sun
And write my love song to the gay skylark;
But I must feed the pigs and milk the cows,
I have more work than I'll get done by dark.

I'd like to write of beauties that I see
In all the little flowers by the lane;
Alas, I must be going on my way,
For it is time to feed the calves again

"Perchance", you say, "The winter brings me ease",
But how can I sit by the fire to write
Or gather inspiration from my dreams
When I should chink the log barn warm and tight?

How can I sit beside the fire at night
And rove with inspiration's lofty bliss,
When there's a little tot named Peggy Mae
Who climbs upon my knee for bye-bye kiss?

(June 8, 1934)

SHE LOVED A DREAMER

"I once loved a dreamer", the lady said,
"And my friends were loud and profane.
They said he'd soon tire of one sweetheart,
And my love would be in vain.

"But I learned how to hold my dreamer,
I shared with him every dream,
And when his dreams were shattered,
I went down with him in the stream.

"Having a dreamer companion,
I oft had but little to eat,
But now that I am old, it won't matter,
For my dreams are young and sweet."

(September 1, 1937)

16

TRUE LOVERS

In youth, they twined their arms about each other,
And smiling, cast their faces to the sun,
Whispering to the little breeze that passed,
That they were always going to live as one.

Oh, how they've loved, these lovers through the years,
As sheltering one another from the cold,
And living there beside the old stone church,
They never once longed to search for gold.

They've been content to live the simple life,
Asking no more than just to be in love,
To be caressed by raindrops from the sky,
And listen to joyful bells from up above.

They've faced the world a life time and grown wise,
These simple lovers, old and brown and tall.
And they shall cling together till the end,
These ivy vines beside the old church wall.

(August 21, 1934)

THE POWER OF LOVE

Of all the powers this great earth enfolds,
Powers of brawn and of brain untold,
From the flapping wing of a fledgeling dove,
To the master minds and the power of gold.

There is nothing can rule the will of man,
Nothing brings him more joy or more strife,
Than the passionate cruel thing called love,
It is the greatest power in life.

Did I say 'twas the greatest power in life?
Did I say 'twas the giver of food and breath?
Wait, I've made a mistake and I ought to know,
For love is itself both life and death.

(February 1935)

UNFAITHFUL

I plucked a summer flower, a rose for you.
I gathered it with morning's sweetest dreams:
'Twas laden then, with gems of sparkling dew,
Where gaily danced the myriad bright sunbeams.

But hours passed, it withered and it died.
It's beauty with the dewdrops, long had fled;
The sun had gone when I sat down and cried:
Knowing full well your love for me was dead.

That wilted rose is now a token dear,
A memory of sweet hours spent with you.
I hold it to my burning lips and hear
Your fervent whisper that you would be true.

(June 1934)

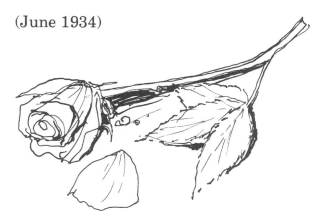

19

A MAN AND HIS MATE

I love you because you kissed me,
I love you because you have trust,
And I live for that consummate meeting,
Which time will come soon, it must.

The angels decreed our obsession;
The Gods gave us faith in our love;
Now we hold full sway and possession
As a nest holds the eggs of a dove.

It's a love made 'neath heaven's great halo,
A bethrothal sanctioned by grace;
That's why we such poor mortals are happy,
For our love conquers darkness and space.

(October 1934)

OLD FOLKS

I know a house on a little old street
In a village that is crumbled with age,
Where life goes on peacefully from day to day,
Where they've never joined in the world's wild rage.

Now in this home lives a woman and man,
And they are mellowed with age and with love,
They have lived in peace for these eighty years;
Their feet on earth and their hearts high above.

The old man still works for the daily bread
While his good wife makes the biscuits and pies;
And if you should travel the world around,
You'll find no more peace 'neath the earth's fair skies.

Now on Saturday night it's a real blessing
To watch them go hand in hand down the street,
For they window shop as they go along,
And they stop to talk with old friends they meet.

And on Sunday morn without halt or fail
You'll find the old folks at the village kirk;
You'll hear them say it is good for their soul
And it helps them to love, and do their work.

LOVE'S ASHES

She was a fire all consuming
Tall, tender, fair as the Scots bluebell
Passionate she, as eternal fire.
Our love reflected both heaven and hell.

Her eyes held the depth of an ocean.
Soft, gentle she, as a dove
But now she is gone, my heart's empty,
I'm alone with the ashes of love.

HEAVEN I SAW

'Twas heaven that I looked upon
Deep down there in your eyes.
I'm sure that it was heaven,
For bright angels filled the skies.
And each angel had a turned up nose
With freckles on her face,
And from all their songs and dancing
I'm sure they liked the place.
There were red rose-covered bowers,
And sands all white and clean.
There were moonbeams on the water,
And great towering evergreens.
But what made me love this paradise
Far more than I could own,
'Twas because I knew that you
Would soon be mine and mine alone.
Answer:
Sure 'twas happiness you gave me,
When you looked into my eyes;
A happiness I shan't forget
While starlight dots the skies.
I remember how the waters glowed
In moonlight's silver sheen,
And although your eyes held mine, I peeped,
And saw the ever-green.
I remember how the raindrops
Fell softly from above,
While softer still your dear, dear voice
Was whispering words of love.
Ah, yes, I loved your paradise,
Way out there in the West,
But of any place or anyone,
'Tis you I love the best.

23

HOUR ALONE

I like to sit at the close of day,
And feel the warm breeze on his homeward way,
And watch the moon in his bower above
Or list' while the doves in the eaves make love.

I like the sound of yon lowing herd,
And the o'erhead whirr of the homing bird.
The distant chimes of the vesper there,
As it calls the faithful to church for prayer.

It is good to see, as I homeward tread,
The sleepy flowers all nod their head,
Hear the tired bee drone in the drowsy dusk,
From his cradled bed on a pile of musk.

There's love in the slap of a wavelets hand,
As he gently chides the moon-splashed sand.
Oh, the thrill of the lark on his heavenward flight,
To snatch the last tendrils of fading light.

Just let me sit when the day is through,
When the robin beds down with his hungry crew.
While the night owl dreams on some ancient spire,
I'll spend this hour in dreams by the fire.

And still to round out this hour bless'd,
Let me hold you dear to my hungry breast
And feel the caress of your lips divine,
'Twould surely be heaven, this hour of mine.

WHERE THERE IS HOPE

I know a cottage where the earth's ends meet,
And 'round that cottage is a garden green,
And 'neath the shady trees there's a road runs down
To where the tranquil harbor can be seen.

And in that cottage, and the garden 'round,
There lives a lady with soft silver hair,
Years hence she told a young man she would wait,
And fifty years now she has waited there.

Her sailor sweetheart clasped her to his breast,
When she was young and beautiful with love,
'Twas then she made the promise that she'd wait;
He pledged true love, while shone the stars above.

She walked with him along the winding trail,
Until his tall white vessel came in sight,
A strange foreboding caused her many a fear;
And thus, in love, they lingered till daylight.

He went then, with her blessing and a smile,
She, turning back then to the cottage, wept;
And many tears she's wept upon the flowers,
And many long dark nights she has not slept.

Her days were spent in hope waiting for him,
And down beside the sea she'd watch for ships;
But to this day his ship has never come.
No lover in these years has kissed her lips.

But she'll be hopeful till the very last,
Though time seems slow, she knows there's not much
    more
Until she too, shall sail an unknown sea
And he will greet her on some distant shore.

THE LOVERS

'Twas by the Mediterranean they were raised,
Where terraced fields slope gently up from sea,
Where gay dressed birds, and songsters worked and sang
Among the grape, and olives green, thick set.
Here Della Yates, a fair Italian girl,
Played with her childhood lover, Walton Zaak.
They built sand castles on the golden shore,
Tall castles which were washed away each night
To be again built up by childish hands,
As are the dreams of men so often wrecked,
Only to be rebuilt time again
As though vain man knew no discouragement.

But lo! the fleeting years passed on their way,
And they from laughing childhood gained their youth,
Yet, as time passed, they seemed to grow more fond,
And Della blushingly took Walton's part
When village folk would idly chaff with her,
And make rude tales about him and his way.

Though Della knew that they were making game,
It pained her gay young heart, and she oft wept,
But she was comforted when he would come
To woo her, kissing all her fears away
And pleasing her with gallant compliment.

Now Della, who, born of a humble home,
Grew beautiful as the fairest flower that lives,
And it was thought by everyone that she
Would someday be the wife of Walton Zaak.
For he was tall and strong, a merchant's son,
Who was well loved by all the village folk,

And it seemed right that these young ones should wed,
So close their young lives had been always linked,
But no man can advance old Fate's decree,
So strongly does he mark the paths of men,
As does the torrent mark the mountain side
Or as a stone will change the brook's smooth course.

Young Walton cherished hopes that some day he
Would own a home, fit for the fairest queen,
And hopefully, he dreamed of Della there,
A jewel placed within a fitting set.
Thus, when a foreign agent told of wealth
In far off Canada, across the sea,
And pictured mansions owned by Italy's sons,
Where gold was lying thick upon the streets,
He was obsessed with keen desire to go
And build the home of which he oft had dreamed.
When all was ready he would send for her
To come and share his luxury and his love.

So when they sat together late that night,
Della, beside him, whispered soft and low,
She told him that she feared their parting thus,
How vividly she pictured their sweet shores,
And, nestling close, spoke of their sacred love,
Till Walton, who had always pleased her, now
Almost gave up his wish to go abroad.
But then ambition ruled his youthful heart
When again, he pictured possible wealth,
And being able to give Della much,
Of comfort she had never known as yet.

But when he told her, Della wept for him,
And tried in vain to make him change his mind,
Both loved old Italy by the tideless sea,

So, Della yielding, gave him her consent,
And hearing his great plans she took new hope.
Then, as the days passed by she planned with him,
And those last days to Della seemed divine,
For hand in hand they walked beside the sea,
Or gamboled, as when children, through the vines.
And her faith in him was doubly renewed,
When, with her small white hand in his strong one,
He oft repeated during those last days,
His love for her, and with a lover's smile,
Oft said that she would never know him gone,
At least would never miss him in the while.

But as the hour of parting came to hand,
Della could not keep from her countenance,
The pain of sorrow bursting her young heart,
And 'twas with heavy step she walked with him
Down to the dock, where his ship's longboat came
To carry him out in harbour where she lay.

Now as the longboat bumped against the dock,
He hurriedly dropped his tiny pack and turned
And taking Della in his arms, he said,
"Wait for me Della, I will come again,
Or send for you to come and be my wife
When I have made a home for you, my dear."
And she, brave girl, kept back a flood of tears,
And kissed him, wishing him a happy voyage,
While painfully she smiled until the boat had drawn
Far out enough that he could not discern,
The tearful anguish on her lovely face;
Then she stood weeping until the boat was gone.

And, turning back, she spent full many days
In praying for his safe voyage and success,

And she more often visited the shrine
Of Christopher, the voyagers' guardian saint.
Then after weeks, a letter came from him,
And though he wrote no disappointing word
She sensed that things were not as he had dreamed,
And that night, through her prayer, an answer came;
She would not wait for him to send for her,
But made resolve to work for peasant wage,
And when enough was saved, she'd go to him.
Together they were sure to make a home
In that new land of distant Canada
For his dear child that she oft prayed to hold.

The ocean voyage had met with fair good luck;
Thus Walton, in short time, saw Montreal,
He left the shipboard in good spirits, and
He walked expectant, gazing on each side,
But failed to find the gold of which he sought.
Then something like a panic gripped his heart
When he realized the folly of his hopes.
He was scant clad for this cold land, and he
Had but a pittance with which food to buy.
And speaking none but his own mother tongue,
Found it most difficult to hold converse.
But even so, the men showed kindly hearts;
They welcomed him to join their company,
And bid him drink a toast to this new land.
Though he knew but a part of what they said,
His lonely heart warmed to their kind intent,
So when with gesture they begged him to sing,
He sang for them a love-song that he knew,
And he was much surprised when it was done
To notice some with teardrops in their eyes,
While others shook his hand and said, "Sing more."

So he sang more, and his sweet song went deep,
And touched the hungry hearts of these rough men,
For in his song the lilting waters laughed,
And birds from their dear motherland sang sweet,
And flowers bloomed beside their distant home,
Where mothers, wives and sweethearts waited them.

When he had ceased his singing and would leave,
Explaining brokenly that he must work,
They laid upon him earnest pleas to stay,
And took up change and paid to him a fee.
So Walton earned a living by his song,
Though it was scant, for those who paid were poor,
But he was proud, and never once complained
Of this new land he'd taken for his own,
And he wrote letters bearing hope to her
Who waited him in sunny Italy.
Though his young heart was often sorely pained
To see how slowly grew his hoard of gold.

Thus crawled the days and months into long years,
Three years, and still he found it hard to save,
But every night he sang upon the street,
And in the barrooms for the food he ate.
And he put all his heart into those songs,
Living each note, each word that left his lips.
For they were words of his dear motherland,
The notes were those he'd sung while still a child,
As now they seemed to warm his hungry heart,
And sent the warm blood gushing through his veins
Where it was needed, for his flesh was cold
From braving winter's cruel sleet and wind.

Now, it was early March that his luck changed,
For, as he sang one night upon the street,

His clear strong voice rang like a silver bell
And it attracted one who knew its worth.
The stranger came to Walton, and he said,
Using the tongue that Walton knew the most,
"Where come you from my lad with such a voice?
Did no one ever tell you that you own
A voice that can be greater than the great?
Come you with me, and I will treat you well,
And in a year, if you will learn from me,
Your name shall be praised higher than the clouds,
And you shall be not only great, but rich,
A singer even greater than 'Caru'."

So, Walton Zaak, trained by a master hand,
Soon gazed upon his name in grand array,
Splashed like a flash of fire across the stage
Before great masses of the idle rich,
Who paid to feel the rapture of his song,
And who were glad to make him one of them.

It should suffice to say that such a rise
Has caused a sterner man to lose his head.
Thus Walton Zaak forgot his former friends,
Carried away by his quick rise to fame,
He fully believed that it would always last,
And it was flattering to one so young,
Having grand ladies seek his company,
So he lived high and kept pace with the throng,
Growing more famous every time he sang,
Until his name became a household word
And where he travelled, crowds would follow him
And wildly shouting, beg him sing for them.

Back home in Italy, among the vines
That grew in terraces beside the sea

Worked Della Yates, keeping her self-sworn vow.
She saved but slowly from the pittance earned,
But if at times she weakened in resolve,
Her will was strengthened when he wrote to her.
Thus she bore on day by slow day until,
The fourth year of her drudgery was at end;
Though now the letters came less frequently,
And they were but evasive notes he sent,
Which bore no single word of his well being,
At last they stopped, and she grew sorely pained,
Fearing the while lest harm should come to him.
So sailed she, not knowing where he'd be,
She trusted Providence to guide her right.

Now when she landed in the land of liberty,
Her young heart thrilled to see his name in lights,
Though she at first could not believe 'twas he,
So sought him where he'd lived in former times,
But after days of fruitless searching him,
She thought at last to ease her aching heart,
By seeing him who bore her lover's name,
The famous one who sang beneath bright lights.
So in the alley by the stage's door,
She waited with the throng who came to stare,
Who, seeing her, moved back and shook their heads,
And wondered why this girl in humble garb
Of foreign peasant, came to gaze on him,
Their idol, yes their idol of the hour,
And it was plain they looked on her with scorn,
And when the stage door opened they forgot,
While clambering to get a better view,
The timid one was nearly trampled down.
Then she saw him, and with much effort came
Forward crying, "Walton! Walton!",

But he passed by, pretending not to hear,
Laughing the while to his gay lady friend,
Then Della, in her weakened state, collapsed,
To later waken in a stranger's house,
Where she'd been carried to receive first aid.

The lady of this house admired the girl,
She hired her as a nursemaid to her child,
Where Della soon learned of the Western ways,
But ne'er forgot the man whom she first loved;
And as a balm to her most wretched heart,
She often bought a gallery seat to hear
And dream the while, that he sang but for her,
As he had done on those far distant shores
Long eons past, when he had claimed to love.

Though Walton had pretended not to see,
He had looked into Della's pleading eyes,
And they now haunted him through day and night,
Then too, he'd find himself comparing her
With these jewelled women who were lax in ways
That he knew Della would not tolerate.
And he could not believe that they were right.
Then he searched for her, but to no avail;
He spoke to no one who had heard of her.
His wish for Della took up all his thought,
So when he failed, a melancholy came
Which settled on him, sapping all his strength
And in this state he took to bed in deep distress.

He all but died, then, rallied back to find
To his dismay that he had lost his voice.
He lost the friends who at his board had ate,
For they now clustered 'round some other light
As moths oft cluster round the candle's flame.

Now in dismay he called on God for help,
And begged the saints to pray for his release.
But the great Master had not deigned it yet,
And he soon walked again for exercise.
While walking through the park one afternoon,
He sat down on a bench to rest the while,
And meditate upon the ways of fate
That deep within his heart he knew were fair.
He knew that he'd been paid in honest coin
So full deserved the punishment he got.
Now gazed he on the greening trees above,
While somewhere in the foliage, hid from view
A thrush piped out his brilliant song of joy,
Just as he'd done so many years ago,
When Walton sat with Della by the sea,
Where he had whispered that he'd always care
While sun and moon shone in the sky above,
But he had failed, he'd been shamed of her
When all was pomp and glory and bright lights;
But he had changed, could God not see he'd changed!

Bowed down in grief he hid his face from view,
To weep for her, whom he had cast aside,
For something in his soul said she'd forgive,
He knew his Della had a heart of gold.
Unworthy as he was, he felt that she
Would understand and take him to her breast.
'Twould seem as if in answer to his prayer,
That Della, on this very afternoon,
Came with her charge, a little boy, to play
And she sat down upon a bench nearby.
She noticed him, this man in fine dark clothes,
Though hid his face, familiar seemed his form,
And Della straightway thought of him she loved

Thus found it hard to take her eyes from him,
So bowed he was in grief apparently,
Though not quite sure, she thought she heard a sob
Then, in a voice she knew so well, her name.

Now all doubt cast aside, she went to him;
She placed her small white hand upon his own,
And said in sweetest voice, "You sick Walton?"
So, taken by surprise, he looked at her,
While tears of anguish still burned his dark eyes,
Seeing him thus, she, without a word
Gently held his head upon her breast.
Not seeing hers, his tears could fall with ease,
For she, too, wept at seeing him so frail,
While in her heart an ancient joy sprang up
At having her own lover in her arms.

When more controlled, he looked at her, and said,
"Forgive me Della, for it is too late;
I've lost my voice, and now I'm poor again,
Not in gold alone, but in losing you.
Fool that I was, in my harsh vanity,
Not to have known that you were meant for me."

Here Della placed her fingers on his lips,
And said, "Hush Walton, do not speak so rash.
Remember what we promised by the sea,
Back home in Italy on the vine clad hill?
You have been ill, my Walton, that is all,
But now you're well, we can resume our plan,
To build a home in this new land of ours."
Then Walton took her in his arms and smiled,
And Della looked up into his eyes.
They kissed, and in one voice, renewed their vow
To live and love as one, until the end.

(November 11, 1933)

People

Photo by John Fairbairn 1972
D'Angelo Portrait Studio

Lyn Kaytor, who was one of John's special friends, has been crippled since birth.

LYN

Nothing is so beautiful as lovely Lyn,
When she smiles
And that alluring little dimple in
The middle of a grin,
That so softly ripples on her happy face at times.

The deep brown bangs match her eyes,
Dancing pools of pure delight.
Her hands say such a lot,
Express such glee.
Everyone's in love with Lyn,
Even me.

FOSTER MOTHER

I know a lady with white hair
A smiling face and deep blue eyes;
She is a flower sweet and rare
An Angel from the clear blue skies.

My mother died before I saw her smile
But still I know she was a princess dear;
She would have cared for me the while
I cling unto her breast in helpless fear.

And then this lady came to helpless me
As I have said, with love's glow on her cheek;
No one more sweet or kind could be
To any child so young, so sick and weak.

And since to manhood I have grown
I love her deep within my humble heart.
She is the mother, that I have known
And I pray that we shall never part.

(June 29, 1934)

SCHOOL MA'AM

She's a simple little school ma'am,
But her kingdom's nation wide,
She has mothered all the nation's men - to - be,
She has taught the greatest sages,
(And she's also tanned their hides)
And her mighty power spreads o'er land and sea.

She's not so much to look at,
But her heart is big and kind,
She isn't heavy jewelled or regal gowned,
Hers is a thankless duty, this gardening of the mind,
For they forget about her kindness,
And remember when she frowned.

But her knowledge and devotion,
When imparted to some kid
Will live on his histry's pages for all time,
For they'll tell about his battles
And the noble things he did,
While the poets set his deeds to glowing rhyme.

And that shabby little laddie
Will become a power on earth,
Just because she helped him cure an awful lisp,
And they'll never give her credit
For one fraction of her worth,
They think their children gained it "will-o-wisp".

But her pay is all in knowing
That she's done a splendid job,
And you ought to see her eyes light up with joy,
When she reads about a hero,
Some young medal-covered "swab",
Whom she taught, when he was "just a little boy".
(November 11, 1940)

41

GREED

Men roam the field and face the flood
For gold, 'til their courage fades;
They waste their youth and their manhood
On the metal which evades.

They spend their time in fighting
Desert storms and winter's blast;
They defy the laws of nature
Until youth and strength have past.

Poets glorify these wastrels
And their great deeds multiply;
These men who hunt cold riches
And never see the summer sky.

They spend their lives in digging
And gloating over gold they get;
They never see the rosebud burst
Or see the bright sunset.

They never hear the bird's sweet song,
These strange men of our race;
They dig the hole into which they fall,
Sans love, sans friend, sans grace.

THE MOST OF US

There's a lot of us who prattle
Over things we call hard luck;
But if the truth were really known,
What we need most is pluck.
We whimper and we dally 'round
Every time the markets fall;
But we never see the beggar,
And we never heed his call.

And we tell a tale pathetic
Of the downfall of mankind;
And we think the country's ruined
When *our* taxes get behind.
We never for a moment dream
That the cause is mostly us,
As we lean upon our shovels,
And kick up clouds of fuss.

Then the dust blots out our vision,
And we mourn an awful pile,
Claiming in a woeful manner,
That this country cramps our style.
That the politics are putrid,
And that life's no longer sure;
But while airing our obsession,
We forget about a cure.

Now what most of us are needing,
As we grouch along our way,
Never heeding lovely flowers,
Or the beauty of the day,
Is someone to see our failings
And point out just where we're wrong.
Teach us to laugh at our failings,
And burst into joyous song.

43   (July 31, 1934)

THE WIFE OF BIG JOE LAKE

A bunch of the boys were playing pool
In a little western town,
While "booze" and jokes and stories
Were bein' passed around.
The wind outside was howling fierce
And the storm was getting bold
A lot of the boys had crowded in
Just to be out of the cold.

Then a blizzard shot from the northern sky,
Like the charge from a cowman's gun,
And to stick your head outside the door
It wasn't what you'd call fun,
But all of a sudden the door went wide,
And in from the driven cold,
Stumbled a pale faced, pretty woman
Who didn't appear very old.

Her eyes seemed wrapped in a misty daze
As she looked around the hall,
Then she staggered, and I grabbed her
For I thought she was gonna fall.
Then they brought her a shot of hard stuff,
Which she gulped with a crazy smile,
And I noticed then that Big Joe Lake
Had been watching her all the while.

In her ragged silk dress she shivered some,
But the drink seemed to bring her back,
She looked over the bunch with a sickly grin,
As she said "One of you skunks is black!
I married one of you lousy lugs,
Left a good home 'way back East,
And I've been cold and whipped and hungry
Since the night of my wedding feast.

"You brought me here to a scrawny shack,
With a pole bunk and rabbits for grub,
When you cinched my love and my money,
You cuffed me around like a cub."
She looked 'round again at the ugly bunch
That hung on her every word,
An' except for her words, the drop of a pin
Could have been easy heard.

Then she cried in a voice that was cold and sharp
As the wind outside the hotel,
"And I know you're a bitch, and I'll shoot you down
For you ought to be in Hell!"
She grabbed my gun from its holster
Before a breath I could take,
And she drilled three holes through the heart
Of the "buster" Big Joe Lake.

She made one leap and she grabbed his gun;
She took his poke and his knife.
She backed her way to the opposite door,
The woman who must'a been Big Joe's wife.
The "cops" they came and took away some clues,
And we buried Joe Lake in the groun';
But from that day to this nothing's ever been heard
Of Joe's wife who shot him down.

(June 28, 1934)

45

BOY BY THE SEA

I like to play beside the sea,
While far on either hand
With friends I play at make believe
'Mong riffles on the sand.

We play at knights and ladies gay
In castles towering high,
And while away the summer's day,
Under the turquoise sky.

I like to play at make believe,
To be a warrior bold,
Or to be a mighty pirate chief,
The white sand my stronghold.

I'd be the terror of the main,
In my ship called "Seafoam".
I'll come to play with you again
But now I must go home.

(September 9, 1934

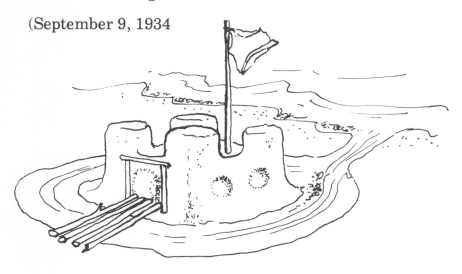

MY OLD CAYUSE

My old cayuse has just now gone
Across the creek without a shore.
I wonder when my turn will come,
It won't be long now, any more.

'Cause I was nigh on forty years
When I caught Bill, then two years old,
And bein' friends for thirty years,
Means I will be soon getting old.

And we've had lovely times, old Bill
And me, aroaming on the range.
There's something in a cowman's life
Which makes him so he will not change.

You know, we've often slept out nights
Beneath bright stars twinkling so,
And Bill was dashed good company
My God, I wish he didn't go.

It makes me awful lonesome now
To think about them days that's past,
But still I guess it's best this way
Than if Old Bill had been the last.

But sunshine don't mean much to me,
And I don't crave a new horse more,
And since Bill's gone there ain't no fun
To dream beside our cabin door.

So I'll be glad when I'm called too
To join Bill on the other side,
And if it won't be breakin' rules
I'll take my cayuse for a ride.

(September 9, 1934

47

POOR BOY

Oh Mom, it would be nice to have that dog,
His fur's so curly and so brown.
Look at his eyes, they're bulgin' almost out,
He'd be the best dog in our town.
Imagine him and me down by the creek,
Or over in McPherson's wood.
If only I could have a dog like that,
I'll betcha I'd be awfully good.

Dad, but it would be great to have that bat,
And that big leather catcher's mitt.
Then if Bill Jones did bat her pretty hard,
I'd just stand there and wait for it;
And we would play down on the vacan' lot,
And if I told you all the truth,
I have ambishums to grow up some day
And be a player like "Babe Ruth".

Oh boy, it would be great to have that gun;
A feller could just knock 'em cold.
And I've been hearing, in the woods back North
The wolves are getting mighty bold.
My Dad was tellin' 'bout a grizzly bear
Which chased a feller up a tree;
I betcha ten bears couldn't make me budge
If I just had that gun with me.

Smoked fish: but that sure is a marv'lous horse;
He ought to be just right to ride.
Now take a look at how he bows his neck,
And all those spots along his side.
If he was mine I'd ride out to some ranch,
And get myself a job to do;

48

I'd live there with the cowboys day and night
Until the round-up was all through.

Some folks think it is sissy to be wishin'
For this and that the live long day;
But Dad says if you keep on wishin'
The wish is bound to come your way.
Of course, he says you've got to work hard, too.
And plan a little 'long the way.
My Dad says, "Spend your spare time wishin'
And when the sun shines, make your hay."

(August 14, 1940)

THE BUM

He's the kind of guy who looks at life
With a cynical sort of an air.
He likes most every man he meets,
But he knows that some can't play fair.

He's fallen in love a number of times,
But his victories have been quite few,
Though he has no quarrel with the other sex
He just knows that they can't be true.

He's made a heap of dough in his time
But he'd rather give than to save.
Though people call him a worthless cuss,
There's some who know he's kind and brave.

He slouches along life's stony road
With but little of which he can boast,
Still I'll bet when he dies he'll be numbered
Up there with the godly host.

THE BIG HOUSE

Tramp - tramp - tramp - they march,
Each prisoner to his lonely cell
In the house of sin and sorrow,
The house of concrete hell.

Plod - plod - plod - they go,
Each gang to their separate block.
Their shepherd is an armed guard
Who hates the sight of his flock.

On - on - on - they grind,
Dragging ball and chain.
Men who have mothers and sweethearts
Who will never see them again.

Thus they must pay in anguish,
They have broken the laws of man,
Here they must rot to pay,
But when they have paid, what then?

Slow - slow - slow - they die.
Hearts grow empty as shells.
Souls grow small and withered and dry;
There is no love in the house of hells.

(July 15, 1934)

BOOZIN' BILL BARNES

Boozin' Bill Barnes was an old cow hand
Who worked on the Bar C Ranch,
Nobody knew 'bout Bill's family tree,
But he was a darned tough branch.
I've seen that cuss eat a raw sparrow—
Gizzard and feathers and all.
We never did think of any bluff
That Boozin' Bill wouldn't call.

When the pay-off came, he'd ride to town,
And he'd booze and squander his "jack".
He'd treat every dance hall girl in the place;
Then broke, he'd come a ridin' back.
I don't think "good folks" like such men,
And they're looked on as so much scum.
But I'm tellin' you folks he was one of the best,
Boozin' Bill wasn't any bum.

There was never a cow man rode a horse
With more guts than Boozin' Bill,
For he'd tackle the very roughest bronk
When he knew he was goin' to spill.
He could bulldog a steer in a real jiffy,
And fight like an old bull moose,
He was always in there pitchin'
Whenever the herd broke loose.

But the reason we liked old Bill so much,
Was because of his great big heart.
He'd risk his life out in a blizzard,
Just to give some new calf a start.
I've seen some young lad fail his watch,
On a cold and stormy night,
And Boozin' Bill was first man there
To carry on the fight.
We'd all seen the kindness quite often,
That was in the heart of Old Bill,
So I guess you can see why we all wept some
When he passed on over the hill.

(July 4, 1935)

IF I WERE JUDGE

I'd never judge folks by the clothes they wear
Or by the cash they have on hand.
Nor would I judge folks by the car they drive
Or their jewels glittering grand.

I'd not judge folks by the church where they pray,
Or donations to charity,
I'd not judge folks by the house where they live,
None of these things mean much to me.

But I would judge folks by the smile they wear,
And the way they treat a hobo.
And it would impress me if I should see
Them take their children where they go.

(October 27, 1934)

53

THE BUM'S LAMENT

Every freight train now is crowded
From her engine to her caboose.
Her passengers are young fellows
Who should be carefree and foot-loose.
Foot-loose they are, you're right at that
But their cares are sad and many,
For they are far from a decent meal,
Scant clothing, and without a penny.

I've watched them come and watched them go;
Two years I've seen mere lads
Beg for just one small bit of lunch.
I've watched fine boys with bringing up
Slip and fall in the rotten slime;
No matter how good a boy has been
"Rubby-Dub" will get him in time.

I want to say, and I ought to know
That hunger will get any man.
Don't take my word, just look around,
There's examples on every hand.
They won't be at the Royal York,
Or in the Chateau Laurier.
The jail house has a bunch of them,
Where they can't see the light of day.

And most of those lads have started small
By stealing grub or a flop,
Or maybe some kind hearted dope fiend
Has given him a shot of "hop".
What started him? I'll tell you what,
He'd come to the end of his rope.

When a boy's hunted work for years,
He's liable to lose every hope.

So come you drinker of red wines,
You men who have a dozen coats,
With bank accounts and limousines
And a million dollars in boats.
Shed of some of your sheckles now.
Pave your way to heaven above.
Show us the stuff we read about,
This kindness and brother love.

(August 18, 1934)

Prairie Wool

SOFTLY IT SNOWS

Softly the snow is coming down,
In tiny flakes that caress,
Surely, but oh so silently,
Earth gets her winter's nightdress.

Now strangely old dreams fill my mind,
My thoughts now drift far away,
To a shanty home old and brown
And a barn that's filled with hay.

I see the soft snow flakes come down
On a pile of drifted leaves,
And there's the impatient twitter
Of sparrows under the eaves.

And there are children looking out
The shanty's lone window pane,
And they are quite pleased I can see,
To welcome winter again.

And as softly the snow comes down,
My eyes fill with lonely tears,
For I know I can only dream
Of those happy childhood years.

(October 24, 1940)

58

AUTUMN

Autumn has come with all its magic glow,
Fairies have dabbed each leaf with brilliant gold,
Red and yellow and brown all in new design,
Cover the glades where green things used to grow.

The wind now rustles through the stubble field,
Where grew a crop of wheat most bountiful;
The rabbit king finds no protecting crown,
He crouches now forlorn without a shield.

Grain wagons rumble over frozen roads,
Reminding one of distant cataracts,
And there is something awesome in the sight
Of horses straining under heavy loads.

High overhead the "Wa-Wa", or wild goose
In mighty wedge-shaped bands cleave greying skies,
An ancient squaw picks frozen chokecherries,
To make big medicine for sick papoose.

With feverish haste, the muskrat works all day,
Laying in stores for winter's endless moons;
Full well he knows that he must work, and fast,
The lake is freezing, there's no time for play.

And now grows cold and damp the northern blast
Storm clouds are gath'ring heavy overhead,
The storm comes, bringing snow in mighty piles,
And now we realize that autumn's past.

(August 3, 1934)

LAND OF CONTRADICTIONS

There's a voice deep down inside me
And it's tugging at my heart,
Saying in a coaxing whisper,
"Boy, you've loved her from the start".

"Why not go?" the voice keeps saying,
"Live out where your heart desires,
Where the crooks are often preachers,
And the 'good men' often liars."

So I'm gonna heed the calling,
Leave this dark and musty clime,
For the land where rains are seldom
And the sun shines all the time.

Out where man is just a mixture
Of the earth and sun and sky,
Where they help you if you need it,
And don't ask the reason why.

Where the heart of every woman
Is a prize men fight to win;
Where life is free and easy,
And they don't call love a sin.

Where the saying, "Live for loving",
Is a twisted little joke,
For 'tis there this love for living,
Will often steal your poke.

Out where man can make a blunder,
And can drink away his thirst,
Where the worst is often better,
And the best is often worst.

So don't bother 'bout the music,
Let me go back to the West,
Let me live and die out yonder,
In that land which God has blessed.

(July 1939)

THE GOOD OLD DAYS

In the good old days, 40 - 30 - 40 was an arm full of pleasing pulchritude.

In the good old days the road to Hell was paved with good intentions. TODAY IT IS A BLACKTOP FREEWAY.

In the good old days, a woman was a rag, a bone and a hank of hair, but then as now, if properly assembled, she makes a very pleasing package.

In the good old days women wore whale bone, and men chewed OLD MARIN SPIKE TOBACCO.

In the good old days it was not so difficult to balance our net income with our gross desire.

CALL OF THE WEST

I am anxious to be goin'
To the place the wind is blowin',
Where the sunshine makes the world look just like gold.
Where the pine trees are a-swayin',
And the bush-wolves are a-bayin',
For upon my lonely heart it's got right hold.

I long to be a talkin'
Or with my ol'mule walkin'
On the moose trail which runs down behind the lake,
And I kind of wish 'twas snowin'
So that I could be a-goin'
Through the woods a-packin' winter's big grub-stake.

Then I'm also kin'a wishin'
That I was goin' a-fishin'
In my little bark canoe on gooseneck stream,
Where the speckled trout are hoppin'
Where the foamy water's choppin'
And just down a bit the rocky rapids scream.

Maybe I'm an awful sap
But I like to hear the yap
Of my husky dogs when it's a-coming dawn,
To pull on my parka hood,
And go out to chop some wood
And there beside my shack to see a fawn.

And then it's kind'a nice
After winter's snow and ice,
To sit beside my shack, in early spring,
And listen to the gopher whistle
Or watch the badger bristle,
And watch the red breast robin build and sing.

That's why I will soon be hikin',
For you'll admit it's strikin',
It's the place of all my plans and all my schemes,
And at night I keep a-thinkin'
Of the little stars a-blinkin'
And the moonlight on the land of all my dreams.

(July 7, 1934)

ELEGY TO THE WEST

Upon the hill I stand and look below
Where once of beauty there was never dearth;
Once myrid flowers grew in gaudy show,
But now the sun shines on a blackened earth.

The bellowing moose call's heard no more,
Now furrows spread before me like a sea,
I hear the distant motor's angry roar,
Then how I wish for things that used to be.

The badger has forsaken ancient haunts,
Cree braves no longer dance beneath the moon,
No longer does the coyote hurl vain taunts,
I never hear the laughing of the loon.

No longer do the shaggy buffalo feast
Upon sweet grasses of ravine and knoll.
There was then mighty herds of this great beast,
But avarice has reaped his deadly toll.

Oh Mother Nature canst thou substitute?
Why should the search for gold seem all worthwhile,
Why should the song of nature be struck mute,
And ghastly furrows ruin earth's sweet smile?

Our plows throw up the bones of "Black-foot" braves,
To bleach or crumble 'neath the cruel sun.
'Tis wrong to desecrate these ancient graves,
Where men have hailed their Gods since time begun.

Where Chippewa squaws once sat before the blaze,
And gossipped peacefully over reeking smoke,
Or watched the papoose romping in the maize,
Our plow does now this sacred earth provoke.

The happy cowboy is now but a memory,
His wild stampede is now almost forgot,
He lived and loved and fought in harmony,
But soon oblivion must be his lot.

Though industry now scorns those awkward times,
I humbly rev'rence those good days so blessed,
And honor them at least in humble rhyme,
The men who caught and tamed the savage West.

(June 6, 1936)

LET ME STAND TALL

Oh Lord make my heart appreciate
The things that are yours and mine.
Don't let me stoop to unworthy thought
Let me stand tall in a world that is fine.

Teach me to love the things You gave.
Never to grumble or whine.
Let me never envy the rich man's way.
Let me learn to value the things that are mine.

Oh Lord, let me feel Your presence near,
On this spot of land you have blessed.
Let me hold what I have in tender love
Let me keep what I have and waive the rest.

Keep me content with the simple life;
Let me love you, God, and my neighbor too,
My children, my home, and my gentle mate.
Let me see all men perfect as you would do.

LAND OF GOD

I'm leaving this big noisy city,
Leaving all this dust and this grime,
I'm grabbing a westbound freight train
I'm going to that bright western clime.

I'm leaving the big noisy city,
Going where God's blessings have smiled,
Where I learned to love the prairie
When I was young and happy and wild.

I'm going to where the pocket-gopher
Sits and whistles all day to the sun,
Out where we shoot the old diamond rattler
Dewy mornings just for fun.

Out where they tend great herds of cattle
All night through the driving storm,
They are wild and rough cow busters,
But they have a heart that is warm.

I am going to build me a cabin
By jumbo hill on the edge of the pine,
I'll farm and raise me some cattle,
And hunt moose up the old timber line.

Then I'll go and get me my sweetheart,
And we'll settle down there with our love,
It's the land of God is the prairie,
With its blue skies and sunshine above.

(October 11, 1937)

PATRIOTISM

WORK FOR WILLIE

I've been wondering and wistful because Willie doesn't
    write,
Though I know he's helping make old England's might,
For my Willie is a gunner, and he's gunning there
    tonight,
And I'm sure what he's doing is what's right.

I can hear the children screaming, and their pitiful wee
    cries,
I can see the wounded mother smile to cheer them as she
    dies,
That's why Willie's up there fighting over London's
    murky skies,
Though they used to think him useless, he's a hero in my
    eyes.

I can see him zooming downward on the tail of some black
    hun,
And my Willie's thinking of it as just so much good fun,
But my Willie doesn't realize this war has just begun,
That's why I'm down and praying for God's blessing on his
    gun.

But when it's all blown over, and the smoke has cleared
    away,
And suppose he's lived right through it and comes back
    again some day,
He can't go on Relief again in the same old rotten way,
There must be work for Willie or there'll be "hell to pay".

(November 9, 1940)

VETERAN

When the jungle grub is rotten
And the bumin's mighty tight,
And the most that you have gotten's
Half enough when it comes night;

When sleet and rain is fallin'
And your rags are wet and froze,
And there ain't no pals a'callin'
And your cold bones start to doze.

When you wake the storm's still groanin',
And there ain't no house in sight,
And your belly's still a'moanin'
For one honest decent bite.

When at home you're no more wanted,
And the road away seems rough,
And from fast'n you're still gaunted,
You'll begin to show your stuff.

Just hitch your belt up with a grin
Walk along and sing and laugh,
Don't give in, it's still worthwhile,
There's been others span the gaff.

(October 6, 1934)

SOLDIER

Down by the sea where the tide comes in,
Drifting with driftwood on the shore,
It is hard to discard the thought of man,
And how he has drenched himself in gore.

It is hard to believe that men can live,
In a world so full of heavenly beauty,
Still rob from another the gift of life
In the name of God and Duty.

Wrapped in the mantle of peaceful dark,
With the song of the ocean in my heart,
It is hard to believe that man with man
Has hated and killed from the very start.

It is hard to believe that under the sun
Man has lost sight of the living God,
Who can curse and kill on the very earth
Where Christ's blessed feet have trod.

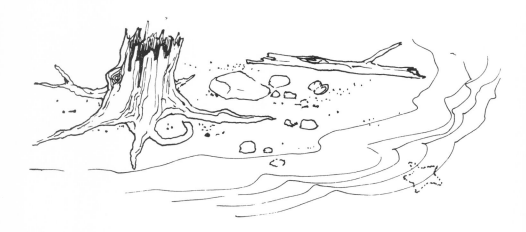

OLD ENGLAND LIVES

Though shells burst on old England's soil,
And England's men die at their toil,
There is a dawn not far away
When she shall know a peaceful day.
Though hatreds now her strength despoil,
"Old England lives."

Though nameless glory sears the sky
Such deeds shall live in days to come.
To save our children and our wives,
For them, and you we gave our lives.
While you fight on through death and rot
"Old England lives."

Though Nations yet unborn must die,
Though round the earth her battle cry
"Democracy must never fail"
Will be our dying deathless wail,
While freedom's banners wave on high.
"Old England lives."

Fight, brother, fight that they might live,
Our life is not too great to give
For those who hold the torch on high
And ever voice our battle cry,
Through gilded castle and through dive
"Old England lives."

(December 5, 1940)

DRAFTED

Softly the white snow flakes
Cast their soothing mantle on my lawn.
Good, bad, and indifferent,
All is now pure and white.
The robin's blood, spilled on the flag-stone path
No longer points like accusing flame
At the striped cat sound asleep in the tree.
The sun's yellow dragon spews scarlet flame
Across the opal and cloud streaked sky.
And the sticky snow on my window sill
Drips tears of anguished pain.
I'm glad snow covers the blood stained path
For it eases the haunting fear that he won't be home,
   Ever again.

ANXIOUS WIFE

Waiting, just waiting for you,
While sinks the sun from sight.
Praying with most of my heart for you,
On through the silent night.

Hoping, just hoping that you
Will come back again to me.
You've done more than I thought you'd do,
You've stolen my heart from me.

That's why I'm alone and weeping for you,
That's why I'm praying this night,
That you'll come back when it's through,
Little Dog from the Big Dogfight.

REFLECTIONS

ANGEL

A sunbeam one bright day was born,
To fade into the shadowed night,
'Twas sadly missed, but it passed on
To somewhere, shed a greater light.

'Twas sadly missed, but have good faith,
God blesses in strange ways;
The little soul in Heaven now dwells,
Thus knowing brighter days.

We must not weep for those He calls,
God chooses those who serve Him best.
Have courage friend; keep fast your faith,
For all good things by Him are blessed.

(November 11, 1940)

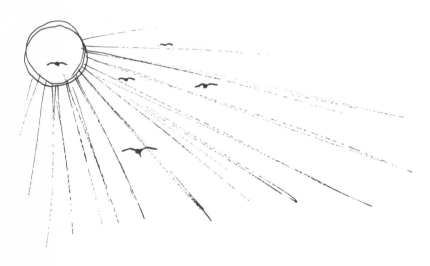

HOPE

A lovely flower,
To bloom unseen behind an ugly pile.
To live an hour;
Then die unloved, a fragrant wasted smile.
Alas, 'twould seem a vain and foolish strife,
A useless beauty, and a wasted life.

A violin,
Of tender tone, played by a master hand,
Drowned in the din
Of blaring trumpets, and a loud brass band.
Alas, 'twould seem a vain and foolish strife
A useless beauty, and a wasted life.

To steal a kiss,
Then find that youth and beauty have both fled;
To capture bliss,
Then realize the one you love, is dead.
Alas, 'twould seem a vain and foolish strife,
But there is God, and His great plan of life.

(December 24, 1940)

SURELY HE SMILED

I've never seen a picture yet
Where He was shown with a smile.
His face is always grave intended,
Surely He smiled once in awhile.

He who loved the little children,
He so human yet so divine,
Surely smiled when some bright laddie
Would 'round His neck wee arms entwine.

Sure He knew happy moments,
Felt joy within His blessed heart,
When on the lake of Galilee
He watched the glorious day depart.

He the Son of God in Heaven,
Loved by so many men on earth,
He who gave his life so bravely,
Must oft have smiled in gentle mirth.

WHEN CHRIST WAS BORN

There is a little town still wrapped in dreams,
Where twinkling stars bedeck the skies at night,
It's been the same, unchanged it seems
Since prophets followed first the bright star light.

The hills around are mantled in soft green,
Where shepherds tend their flocks through endless age.
The ancient wells are as they've always been,
Since first they quenched the thirst of saint and sage.

The pilgrims still come down to Bethlehem
To buy or barter on the village square.
This ancient village is still dear to them,
For here was born of God the Christ Child fair.

The crumbling walls remind them of that day
When heralds claimed a King was newly born.
Then all the land rejoiced, and they were gay
As we rejoice today on Christmas morn.

(July 30, 1934)

83

DEPRESSION

Now most of us whine quite a bit,
And grumble about our lot;
We kick about the things we have,
And want all the things we have not.

We find much pleasure in blowing off
A great cloud of idle steam,
Complaining to folks around us
About our long lost dream.

We spread the old hard luck yarn,
And we cuddle our glooms and fears;
We pull a face as long as your arm
For it's quite becoming to tears.

And talk about tears, we've sure shed some
Since back there in twenty-nine,
Salt tears were then very much in style,
And we soaked ourselves in the brine.

But I'm sure that most of us could find
A fair good reason to smile.
I'm sure if we looked around a bit,
We'd find life quite worth the while.

Now take, for example, the sunshine;
It's been with us through the years.
It's glad and willing to warm our hearts,
And dry away all our tears.

We still have the glorious evening sky,
We still have the moon's soft light,
We still have the little stars above
That twinkle and dance all night.

We have the birdsong and the bees' soft drone,
And we still have the bright bluebell.
The kiss of the breeze will be ours always;
It's something no man can sell.

And besides all these, there is something else
Should bring a smile to our lips.
We have vast riches in friendship's vault,
Right here at our finger tips.

And we can pray if we want to pray,
And thank God for all of these joys,
And we can pass the word right along
To the rest of the tearful boys.

HERITAGE OF PEACE

Deep in a hollow tree they dwell,
Out in the forest green and still,
Far from all human noise and strife,
Far from the men who lust to kill.

Here 'neath a friendly jewel-decked sky,
With but a hollow tree as home.
They live in peace from day to day,
Close to the fragrant scented loom.

On this enchanted spot are found,
The things that all great nations seek;
Here peace and happiness abide,
And here the strong protect the weak.

This home is peopled by wee squirrels
Whom, it is plain to see are wise.
And if they knew our fears and doubts,
I'm sure they'd try to sympathize.

SAILING SHIP

Long she has served and faithfully,
Never betraying a trust.
Through years of gales at sea
She's been brave and strong and just.

Now they've made her into a "tramp-ship",
Stripping her rigging and sail,
She's a lame but noble relic
Who a thousand times stood the gale.

Though she's just a queen in exile,
Romance in her heart runs high;
Served both pirate and prince has she
With her proud sails in the sky.

Though she's now just an "old ship",
All smeared with black coal dust,
She will serve her master faithfully,
And will never betray a trust.

(October 26, 1939)

QUAND'RY

Days come and go like seconds
And lo, the fleeting years
Pass, as do our nightly dreams
Leaving sweet joy, or tears.

Tender saplings by the lane
Have grown, it seems since morn
To be great towering oak trees
Where myriad songs are born.

We live t'would seem, for nothing
But to be born and die
As do bright flowers fade
And breezes pass right by.

Young lips once kissed grow cold,
Youth fades like evening light.
It would seem that dawn of day,
Comes just to bring the night.

Whatever is it all about?
Is this a trial flight?
A journey thro' the darkness
To yonder golden light?

(October 3, 1940)

THE TRAPPER'S DREAM

Let me build a shack some place out west,
By the edge of a river among the pines
Or the side of a lake where loons will laugh,
Or out on some knoll where the bright sun shines.
But no matter where I should build my shack,
Let it be in some quiet natural place,
Where the only noise will be nature's song,
Where the earth will wear a smile on her face.

And 'round my shack in this natural place
I'd like some roses and lillies to grow,
And here and there in the garden patch
I'd like some of them flowers white as snow.
And to cover the bark on my log shack
Give me some vines with the wee yellow buds,
And behind the house where it's shaded well,
There'll be things to eat, like turnips and spuds.

Inside my shack, and I blush to tell,
Will be the girl I've loved for so long;
And just like she did in our courting days,
She'll sing some nice, kinda touchy song.
She won't be singing, of course, just for me,
There'll be a girl baby with her smile.
Oops! It's daylight, guess I'd better get up,
Today's march will be about fifty mile.

(October 10, 1934)

LIFE'S JOKER CARD

As youth's hot passions cool to saner heat,
I look with calmer sight upon the earth.
And wonder if the ecstasy of first young love
Is bought at price far greater than its worth.

I cannot help but feel, at times,
As I gaze into hearts struck sick with strife,
That love is just the joker card
In this great gamble game called Life.

And yet where is the man who lives to say
That he has not won something from the game,
And where's the man who's lost, and will not own
That he, himself, is the one man to blame?

(July 1935)

THE DREAMER

I'm a dreamer can't you see,
I build dream castles high,
I'm richer than most mortals be,
I have the sun and sky.

The silvery moonbeams are all mine,
I have the rainbow's gold;
Rose petals and a warming love,
Sweet dreams for when I'm old.

THE OLD HOME

I am lonesome today for the old rustic shack,
With wide covered porch, by the railroad track.
I am lonesome to tread the old board walk,
There by the trellis where birds used to flock.

In the rose covered arbor I'd like to sit,
Where my dear old Mother long sat to knit.
Or I'd like to stroll by the old stone well
And dream of the stories Grandpa used to tell.

I'd like to pray by the old rocking chair,
Then go off to bed up the short narrow stair.
But alas, I am far from the dear homely shack,
And only in dreams can I ever go back.

WHEN I AM OLD

When I am old, I'll be content to wait
Unmoved beside the fireplace with my thought.
To those who ask, I will be pleased to tell
Just how to solve the problems they have got.
For surely after years of learning life,
I should be very wise and know a lot.

When I am old, and nearing close of day
I'll be content to watch the world rush by.
Let others run and fight whoever will.
I will look on with lifted brows and sigh,
And whisper to myself, "I wish they be
One half as happy and content as I".

DARKNESS

The waning day is giving place
To night, with shadows deep and gray;
And in the deepest shades of night,
Is where, I'm told, man learns to pray.

'Tis then man's heart gains sweet surcease
From troubles of the busy day,
And he can rest in well earned peace,
Where fears and worries drift away.

The solitary owl, and wise,
Will not disturb his reverie;
The glitt'ring stars will watch, but they
Will watch and very silent be.

For have not all great men at times
Felt earnest need of solitude;
And crept away at times to think,
And welcomed nights dark fortitude.

When greatest grief descends on man,
He'll cast his frame upon the sod;
And there in utter darkness pray,
And beg the blessing of his God.

RICHES

"I was rich," said he, "And it sure was fine,
Out of poverty black and sad,
To claim anything as mine,
Forgetting the friends that I had.

"My love too, was mad and selfish,
Sweeping all things from its way,
Oh! but fortune can also be selfish,
For I'm poor and alone today.

"It pays, I have learned, to be giving,
For we get just about as we give,
It pays to be kind and forgiving,
And living, let other men live."

(February 11, 1935)

HOPE RENEWED,

I wandered down by the river last night
Where the banks were shadowed by spray.
I was fed up with this life and the world
And hoping I'd die before day.

Then sitting me down to rest for a while,
I must have dreamed; for standing there
Was a fairy smiling and beautiful
With a halo around her hair.

And she said to me in a kindly voice,
"Come and I will show you about".
"I'm sure", she said, "you will be glad when you see
And you'll lose all your fear and doubt".

Then she led me over the silent fields
To a moonlit nook by a spring.
Then she cautioned me to listen the while
To the sweet lilting waters sing.

Then we saw a little log cabin home.
And around an old stone fireplace,
Sat a man and his wife and their children
Each with a smiling happy face.

Farther on, men and women were working,
And we saw some children at play.
The fairy left me alone, then whispering,
"Now, I hope you have found the way".

I awakened then with a sudden start
The darkness had stolen away
Still the foamy river was dashing on
But now sunlight danced on the spray.

I had forgotten my sorrow and fear,
I was filled with bright hopes anew.
The rosebuds were smiling again for me;
I was ready to dare and do.

(October 2, 1934)

Irene Kelly-Thompson became blind suddenly at the age of 62 in June 1959. Her life had been very active and filled with responsibility. In her early years, she held responsible positions heading the Millinery, Ready-to-Wear and Fur Departments in a large department store in Edmonton.

After being widowed in 1939, Irene trained as a nurse and held positions in Vancouver, the Okanagan and Calgary. As a nurse, she felt the need to provide a good home for the elderly where they could receive the best of food and care in a homelike atmosphere. She purchased a house, and provided this type of care to 10 ladies for five years.

In June of 1959, an unfortunate fall instantly caused her to become blind. She carried on with the home for the elderly for two more years, and hired cooks and housekeepers. It became more and more difficult to get reliable help, she had to give up the project.

Irene then felt that she lacked a purpose in life, and she became very thin, discouraged, and sick. She felt that life had nothing more to offer her. It was at this low ebb in her life that she met John Fairbairn in 1961.

IRENE THOMPSON 1977
photo by D'Angelo Portrait Studio

I felt it was providential that I met John Fairbairn at this critical time in my life when I had lost all purpose and desire to live. I had lost all interest in anybody or anything.

John spent many hours with me in helping to change my whole attitude. He inspired me to use a positive rather than a negative approach to life. Sometimes he got a little rough with me, but I knew it was for my own good. He did more than anyone else to get me back on my feet and to enjoy life again.

Now I live a very normal life. Even though I am blind, I do my own housework and cooking, entertain guests as usual, attend the occasional banquet, and even travel alone by taxi, bus and plane. I am 80 years of age, been blind for 18 years and a widow for 38 years.

It has been three years since John passed away, but his inspiration still lives with me. I trust this message and the poems in this book may provide some encouragement to others who may have given up living because of some handicap or hardship.